N

Is for Nativity

Christmas from A to Z

Written by
Ruth E. Meyer

CONCORDIA PUBLISHING HOUSE · SAINT LOUIS

Advent is our letter **A**, a fitting place to start.

For these four weeks, our prayer is this: "O Lord, prepare my heart."

And now, for letter **B**, we come to **B**ethlehem of old.

Here Christ was born, just as the prophet Micah had foretold.

C is for the heavenly **C**horus singing in the sky.

They told of Jesus' birth and sang, "Glory to God on high."

D is for the **D**reams in which an angel did appear
To tell God's people of His plan and bid them not to fear.

E is for **E**mmanuel, and in this name, we find
It means, "God with us." Christ was born for all of humankind.

The **F**amily line of Jesus hails from Bethlehem.

He's of King David's royal line, the shoot of Jesse's stem.

Our letter **G** is **G**abriel, a special angel who
Brought news to Zechariah and the Virgin Mary too.

H is for King **H**erod, a cruel and evil man
Whose plot to harm the newborn babe could not destroy God's plan.

I is for a special word that's called the Incarnation.
God the Son took on our flesh to earn for us salvation.

Jesus' earthly father's name was **J**oseph, who is **J**.

In faith, he heard the angel's words and hastened to obey.

K is for our newborn **K**ing, who left His throne above
To dwell as man with us on earth because of God's great love.

Scripture gives us two recountings of the first Noel.

One we read in Matthew, one in Luke, which is our **L.**

M is for the **M**anger where the infant Lord was laid.

There was no room in any inn. A stable's where He stayed.

N is for **Nativity**, another name for birth.

When Christ was born, our Lord began His human life on earth.

O is for an **Order** that a census would take place,

So Christ was born in Bethlehem to save our fallen race.

P points to the **P**rophecies, which all proved to be true.
In Jesus Christ, they are fulfilled, for He was born for you.

While Caesar ruled the Roman world with a mighty hand,
Q is for **Quirinius**, who governed in the land.

R reminds us to **R**ejoice for all our God has done.

For God so loved the world, He gave His one and only Son.

S is for the **S**hepherds, who at the angel's word

Saw Jesus Christ, then spread the news of all they'd seen and heard.

T is for the **T**emple, where a man named Simeon saw
The infant Lord, who went there to fulfill Mosaic Law.

A gift is **Undeserved**, our **U**. In Christmas, we are shown
That Jesus is the greatest gift the world has ever known.

V is for the **V**irgin Mary. In her womb, she bore
The baby Jesus. He's the Lord we worship and adore.

Our **W**, the **W**ise Men, were not there on Christmas night.
They came when Christ was older, guided by His star's bright light.

X is for the e**X**odus to Egypt, where we see

That God kept Jesus safe and fulfilled a prophecy.

Old Testament believers waited; **Y** brings us to **Y**earn.

They yearned for their Messiah's birth; we long for His return.

Zechariah is our **Z**. His son grew up to share
That Jesus Christ had come to earth for people everywhere.

Glossary

Advent: The word *Advent* comes from the Latin word *adventus*, which means "coming." Advent is the first season of the Church Year. Beginning the fourth Sunday before Christmas, Advent is a time of inward preparation and waiting for Christ's coming at Christmas and His second coming on the Last Day.

Bethlehem: Micah 5:2 prophesied that the Messiah would be born in Bethlehem. Joseph and Mary lived in Nazareth, but they were required to travel to the town of Joseph's ancestry for a census shortly before Jesus was born. Since Joseph was a descendant of King David, he had to return to David's city, which was Bethlehem.

Chorus: After Jesus was born, an angel appeared to the shepherds to tell them where to find the newborn Savior. Then a "multitude of the heavenly host" appeared, singing, "Glory to God in the highest, and on earth peace among those with whom He is pleased!" (Luke 2:13–14).

Dreams: God sent angels to communicate through dreams many times throughout the Christmas account. An angel told Joseph to marry Mary (see Matthew 1:20–23). An angel warned the Wise Men not to return to Herod (see Matthew 2:12). An angel instructed Joseph to flee to Egypt (see Matthew 2:13), when it was safe to return (see Matthew 2:20), and to live in the district of Galilee (see Matthew 2:22).

Emmanuel: The name *Emmanuel* (or *Immanuel*) comes from Isaiah 7:14, where we read, "The virgin shall conceive and bear a son, and shall call His name Immanuel." Years later, the Virgin Mary conceived and gave birth to Jesus, who is both true God and true man. Indeed, Jesus is "God with us," our Emmanuel.

Family: Scripture foretold that a Savior would come from the royal line of King David. Isaiah 11:1 prophesies that a shoot would come from the stump of Jesse (David's father). Matthew and Luke both record Jesus' genealogy to show that His earthly father, Joseph, was a descendant of King David.

Gabriel: The angel Gabriel appeared to both Zechariah (see Luke 1:8–23) and Mary (see Luke 1:26–38) to tell them of two miraculous births (John the Baptist and Jesus, respectively). Matthew records multiple instances of "an angel of the Lord" appearing in a dream, which could be Gabriel as well, though we cannot know for certain.

Herod: Herod "the Great" was the king of Judea from 40 BC until shortly after Jesus' birth. He was jealous and paranoid of potential rivals to the throne. When the Wise Men asked Herod where to find the "king of the Jews," he plotted to kill this new rival. The account is found in Matthew 2:1–18.

Incarnation: The word *incarnation* means "taking on flesh." We read in John 1:14, "The Word became flesh and dwelt among us." Jesus, the Second Person of the Trinity, became man in order to save us. This incarnation is the focus of our Christmas celebration.

Joseph: Joseph, a carpenter from Nazareth, married the Virgin Mary and raised Jesus as his son. Matthew's account of the Christmas story records four times an angel appeared to Joseph. Joseph listened and obeyed without question each time. He was a godly man who served well as Jesus' earthly father.

King: The Bible often refers to Jesus as our "king" (e.g., Jeremiah 23:5; Matthew 2:2; Luke 19:38; 1 Timothy 1:17; and Revelation 19:16). But Jesus was not born to be an earthly king. He is our heavenly King, reigning over His kingdom, the Church. When Jesus returns, He will reign as King over His entire creation eternally.

Luke: There are two Gospel accounts of the Christmas story—one in Matthew and the other in Luke. Each divinely inspired account records slightly different events. By studying both, we get a more detailed understanding of all that took place that first Christmas.

Manger: Since Bethlehem was crowded for the census, there were few lodging options suitable for a woman giving birth. Mary and Joseph ended up in a stable, which may have been the first floor of a house where families would keep their animals safe overnight. It was warm and private, and Jesus' first bed was a manger, a feeding trough for animals.

Nativity: *Nativity* is another word for "birth." Nativity scenes are paintings or sets with figurines that portray the circumstances of that